Contents

2 times table   4

10 times table   11

5 times table   15

2 and 5 times table   23

Mixed practice   24

How to be a times tables detective!

Times tables are full of patterns and connections. If you know these, it will help you to remember the times tables. It will also help you to use the tables to solve problems and to reason about numbers. There are detectives in this book who will help you to spot patterns. They will also sometimes ask a question to challenge you. When you spot a detective, take the chance to think in a bit more depth, and become a times tables detective!

T Count on in 2s and fill in the boxes.

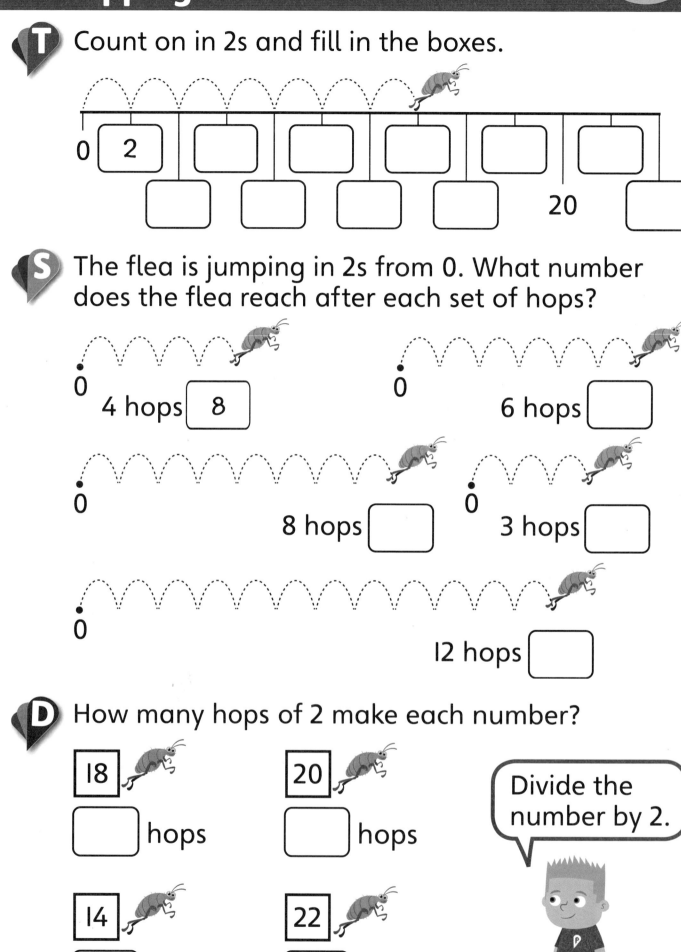

| 0 | 2 | | | | | |

| | | | | 20 | |

S The flea is jumping in 2s from 0. What number does the flea reach after each set of hops?

0
4 hops 8

0
6 hops

0
8 hops

0
3 hops

0
12 hops

D How many hops of 2 make each number?

18
☐ hops

20
☐ hops

Divide the number by 2.

14
☐ hops

22
☐ hops

Car parks

 T Write a ×2 fact to show the number of cars.

[4] × 2 = [8]   [ ] × 2 = [ ]   [ ] × 2 = [ ]

[ ] × 2 = [ ]   [ ] × 2 = [ ]   [ ] × 2 = [ ]

 S Draw 2 equal rows of dots to match each ×2 fact. Then fill in the missing numbers.

    [ ]   [ ]

2 × 2 = [ ]   6 × 2 = [ ]   11 × 2 = [ ]

 D Draw each number as rows of dots. Then write the matching ÷2 fact.

6   8 [ ]

[6] ÷ 2 = [3]   [ ] ÷ 2 = [ ]

14 [ ]   18 [ ]

[ ] ÷ 2 = [ ]   [ ] ÷ 2 = [ ]

5

T Colour in this block diagram for the ×2 table.

 Each column will have 2 more blocks than the one before.

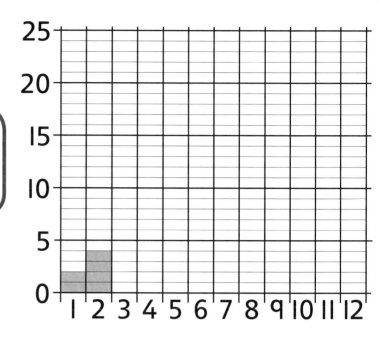

 **S** Fill in the missing numbers.

1 × 2 = ☐   3 × 2 = ☐   6 × 2 = ☐

+ 4 × 2 = ☐   + 7 × 2 = ☐   + 2 × 2 = ☐
────   ────   ────
5 × 2 = ☐   10 × 2 = ☐   8 × 2 = ☐
────   ────   ────

What do you notice about the answer to each question?

D Fill in the part-whole models.

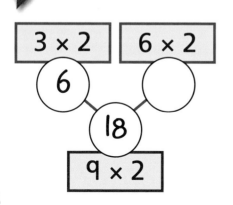

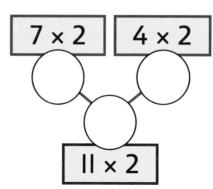

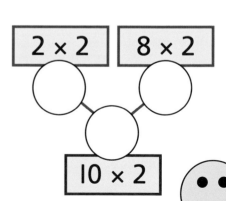

6

Double trouble

T Write the numbers that come out of the function machines.

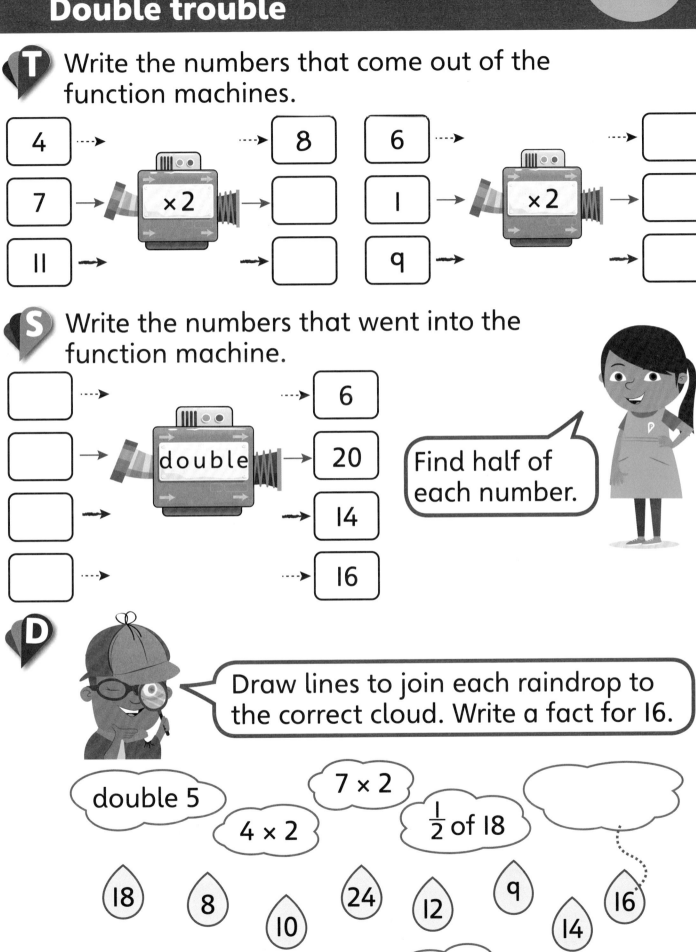

4 ---> [×2] ---> 8

7 ---> [×2] ---> ☐

11 ---> ---> ☐

6 ---> [×2] ---> ☐

1 ---> [×2] ---> ☐

9 ---> ---> ☐

S Write the numbers that went into the function machine.

☐ ---> [double] ---> 6

☐ ---> [double] ---> 20

☐ ---> ---> 14

☐ ---> ---> 16

Find half of each number.

D Draw lines to join each raindrop to the correct cloud. Write a fact for 16.

double 5   7 × 2   ½ of 18

4 × 2

18   8   24   12   9   16

10   14

half of 16   12 × 2

double 9   half of 24

7

Double or halve

×2

T Write the answers on the signs.

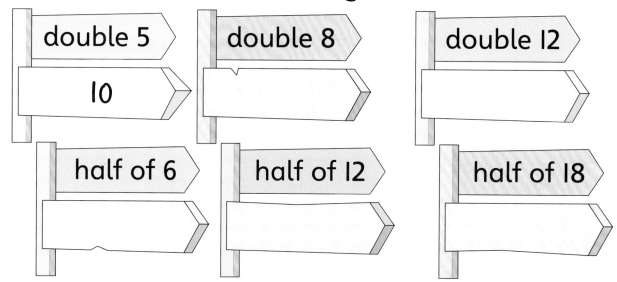

double 5
10

double 8

double 12

half of 6

half of 12

half of 18

S Double or halve the numbers to complete the table.

Half	2	7	8	1	12	5				
Double	4						10	12	20	8	18

What is special about the numbers in the second row of the table?

D Make correct number sentences with these cards. How many can you make?

×2   ½ of   ÷2   =   16   8   4   2   1

_____ _____ _____

_____ _____ _____

_____ _____ _____

×2 fact finders

T Draw lines to join each kite to its owner.

5 × 2   11 × 2   9 × 2   6 × 2   4 × 2   7 × 2

10   18   22   14   12   8

S Fill in the numbers to show the ×2 table facts.

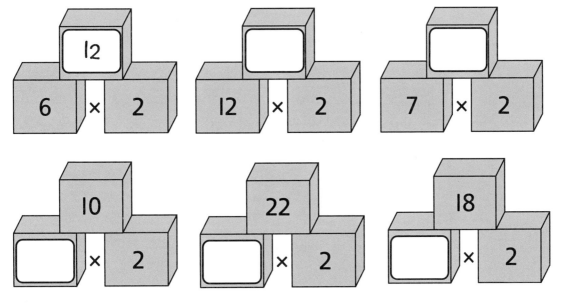

12 │ 6 × 2

☐ │ 12 × 2

☐ │ 7 × 2

10 │ ☐ × 2

22 │ ☐ × 2

18 │ ☐ × 2

Multiply the numbers in the bottom row to make the number on the top row.

D Write a ÷2 fact using the numbers on the blocks. Choose your own numbers for the empty blocks.

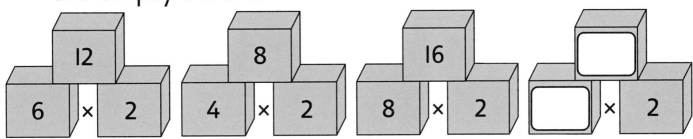

12 │ 6 × 2

8 │ 4 × 2

16 │ 8 × 2

☐ │ ☐ × 2

_____   _____   _____   _____

T Write a ×2 and ÷2 fact for each diagram.

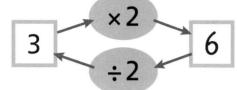

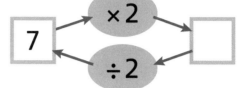

☐ × 2 = ☐

☐ ÷ 2 = ☐

☐ × 2 = ☐

☐ ÷ 2 = ☐

S Find the numbers hidden by the paw prints.

6 × 2 = ☐

1 × 2 = ☐

☐ ÷ 2 = 4

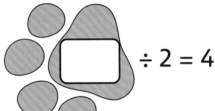

☐ × 2 = 14

☐ × 2 = 22

> Check each fact to make sure it is true.

10 ÷ 2 = ☐

2 ÷ 2 = ☐

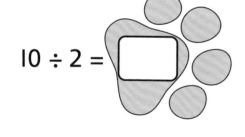
☐ ÷ 2 = 8

D Choose a number between 8 and 12. Write a ×2 fact and a ÷2 fact with the number. Do this three times.

_____ _____ _____

_____ _____ _____

> What do you notice about the first number in each division fact?

T There are 10 seeds in each pot. Write an addition sentence for each group of pots.

3 pots

| 10 | + | 10 | + | 10 | = | 30 |

4 pots

☐ + ☐ + ☐ + ☐ = ☐

5 pots

☐ + ☐ + ☐ + ☐ + ☐ = ☐

S There are 10 seeds in each pot. How many seeds are there altogether in each group?

Point to each pot and count in 10s.

 ☐

 ☐

 ☐

 ☐

D There are 10 seeds in a pot. Complete the tables.

Number of pots	1	2	3	4	5	6
Number of seeds			30			

Number of pots	7	8	9	10	11	12
Number of seeds						

What patterns do you notice?

11

Multiples of 10

×10

T Count in 10s from 0 to escape the maze.
Draw the path you take.

Start by crossing out numbers
that are not multiples of 10.

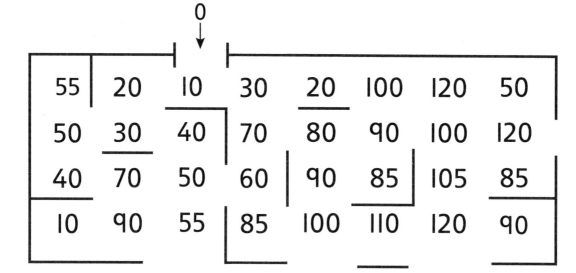

0

55	20	10	30	20	100	120	50
50	30	40	70	80	90	100	120
40	70	50	60	90	85	105	85
10	90	55	85	100	110	120	90

S Colour all the multiples of 10.

Which multiple
of 10 is missing?

15   30   100   51   120   50

48   90   110   80   105

40   10   44   70   20   75

D Choose some multiples of 10. Write a ×10 fact
for each multiple.

[ ] × 10 = [ ]   [ ] × 10 = [ ]

[ ] × 10 = [ ]   [ ] × 10 = [ ]

[ ] × 10 = [ ]   [15] × 10 = [ ]

10p calculations

 Each coin is 10p. How much money is in each pile?

 `30` p    ⬜ p    ⬜ p

 ⬜ p    ⬜ p   ⬜ p

 Each purse holds only 10p coins. How many 10p coins are in each purse?

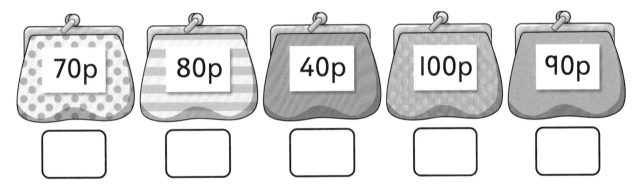

70p	80p	40p	100p	90p
⬜	⬜	⬜	⬜	⬜

D Join each jar to its correct money box.

100 ÷ 10   80 ÷ 10   70 ÷ 10   10 ÷ 10

 10   11   1   7

4   8   9   12

90 ÷ 10   40 ÷ 10   120 ÷ 10   110 ÷ 10

T Tick the correct number sentences. Cross the incorrect ones and write them correctly.

7 × 10 = 70 ✓

11 × 10 = 101 ☐

_____

_____

5 × 10 = 55 ☐

9 × 10 = 90 ☐

_____

_____

1 × 10 = 1 ☐

12 × 10 = 120 ☐

_____

_____

 S Are these statements true or false? Write a number sentence for each one to prove your answer.

When any whole number is divided by 10 the answer always ends in zero.

When any whole number is multiplied by 10 the answer always ends in zero.

_____

_____

 D Write at least 8 facts using these cards. You can use a card more than once.

= 0 1 2 ×10 ÷10

_____ _____ _____

_____ _____ _____

_____ _____ _____

T Count on in 5s and fill in the missing numbers.

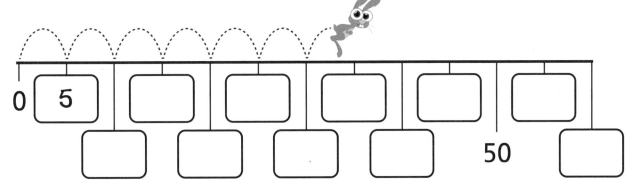

0 | 5 | | | | |

| | | | 50 |

S Multiply each number by 5.

Count on in 5s if you need to.

3 → 15   2 → [ ]   5 → [ ]   6 → [ ]

8 → [ ]   9 → [ ]   11 → [ ]   7 → [ ]

D Colour each multiplication and its answer in the same colour. Use a different colour for each pair.

4 × 5	9 × 5	7 × 5
6 × 5	11 × 5	8 × 5
5 × 5	3 × 5	12 × 5

55	51	42	45
15	60	35	20
25	47	40	30

Which numbers do not have a matching multiplication?

T Circle the correct number of dice to match the dots to the number below.

> Think how many 5s are in each number.

15　　　　20　　　　10　　　　30

S 5 × 5 = 25. Use this fact to find the answers to the multiplications.

| 7 × 5 | 8 × 5 | 9 × 5 |

25 + ☐ = ☐　　　25 + ☐ = ☐　　　25 + ☐ = ☐

D Fill in the missing numbers.

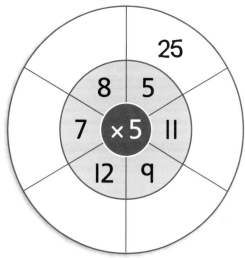

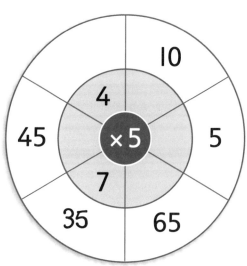

5p calculations

×5

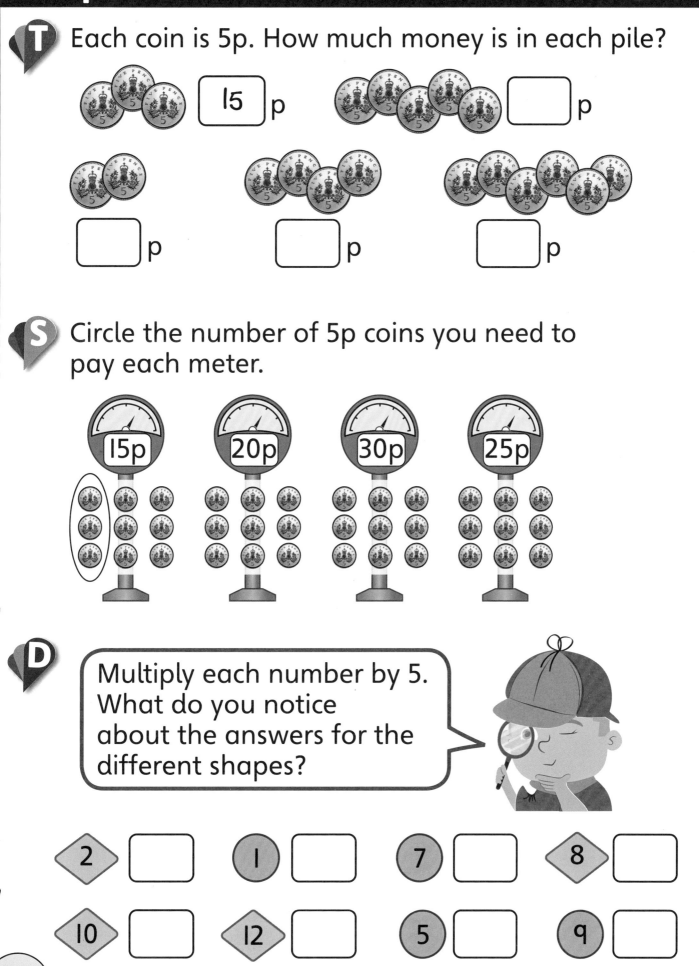

T Each coin is 5p. How much money is in each pile?

15 p

☐ p

☐ p

☐ p

☐ p

S Circle the number of 5p coins you need to pay each meter.

15p 20p 30p 25p

D Multiply each number by 5. What do you notice about the answers for the different shapes?

2 ☐ 1 ☐ 7 ☐ 8 ☐

10 ☐ 12 ☐ 5 ☐ 9 ☐

17

T Complete the spiral of stars.

Count back in 5s.

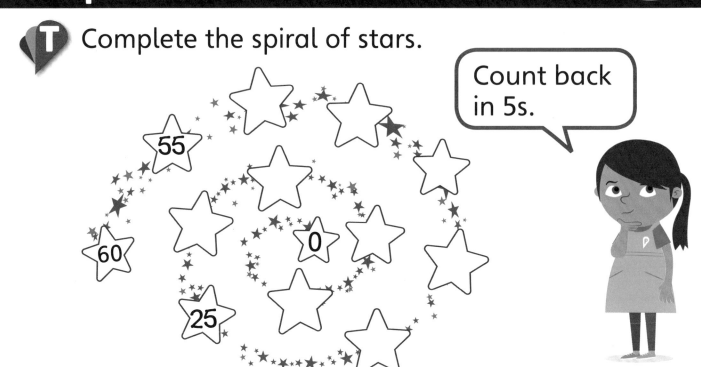

S How many jumps of 5 must each spaceship take to reach the zero star?

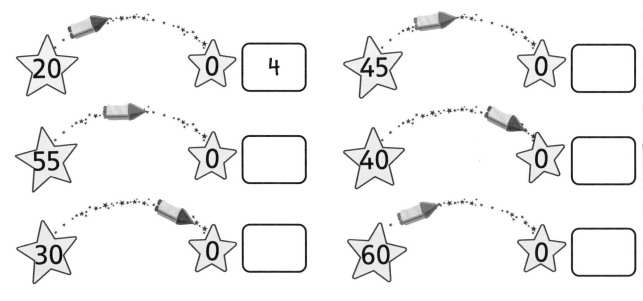

20 → 0 [4]   45 → 0 [ ]

55 → 0 [ ]   40 → 0 [ ]

30 → 0 [ ]   60 → 0 [ ]

D Fill in the missing numbers. Draw a line to join sentences with the same missing number.

$30 \div 5 = \boxed{}$ $45 \div 5 = \boxed{}$ $55 \div 5 = \boxed{}$

$35 \div 5 = \boxed{}$ $\boxed{} \times 5 = 30$ $\boxed{} \times 5 = 40$

$\boxed{} \times 5 = 45$ $\boxed{} \times 5 = 55$ $\boxed{} \times 5 = 65$

How many sweets are there in each group?

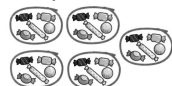   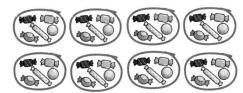

| 5 | groups of 5 = [ ]   [ ] groups of 5 = [ ]

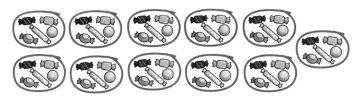

[ ] groups of 5 = [ ]

 Circle groups of 5 dots. Write the divisions to show the number of groups of 5 in each set.

35 dots   45 dots

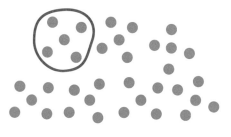   

35 ÷ [ ] = [ ]   [ ] ÷ 5 = [ ]

30 sweets are shared equally so that each child gets 5 sweets. Each child eats 3 of their sweets. How many sweets are there now?

_____

_____

Hands and feet

 T Write a multiplication fact about the fingers and thumbs in each set of hands.

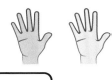 How many hands are there? How many fingers and thumbs?

$4 \times 5 = 20$ $\boxed{} \times 5 = \boxed{}$

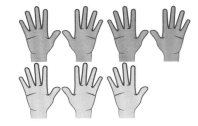

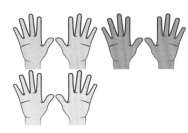

$\boxed{} \times 5 = \boxed{}$ $\boxed{} \times 5 = \boxed{}$

 S Write the ×5 fact about the toes in each set of feet. Then write it as a division fact.

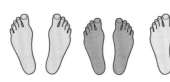

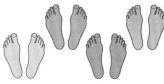

$5 \times 5 = 25$ $1 \times 5 = \boxed{}$ $8 \times 5 = \boxed{}$

$25 \div 5 = 5$ $\boxed{} \div 5 = \boxed{}$ $\boxed{} \div 5 = \boxed{}$

 D Colour the feet that have a correct number sentence. Write the correct answer for the others.

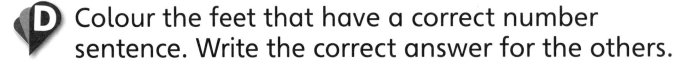

$40 \div 5 = 8$ ☐ $30 \div 5 = 6$ ☐ $55 \div 5 = 11$ ☐

$45 \div 5 = 7$ ☐ $60 \div 5 = 12$ ☐ $15 \div 5 = 3$ ☐

$35 \div 5 = 8$ ☐ $25 \div 5 = 5$ ☐ $20 \div 5 = 3$ ☐

×5 problems

 Draw lines to join each dog to its owner.

8 × 5   9 × 5   6 × 5   3 × 5   7 × 5   4 × 5

15   35   45   40   20   30

 Fill in the missing numbers.

4 × 5 = ☐   ☐ × 5 = 25   1 × ☐ = 5

☐ × 5 = 15   10 × ☐ = 50   11 × 5 = ☐

8 × ☐ = 40   ☐ × 5 = 30   ☐ × 5 = 45

55 ÷ 5 = 11. This fact uses only the digits 1 and 5. Can you write a ÷5 fact using only the digits below? Give examples when it is possible.

2, 5 _____   4, 5 _____

1, 0, 5 _____   3, 0, 5 _____

Cube divisions

T How many groups of 5 cubes can you make from each number?

> There are two 5s in every 10.

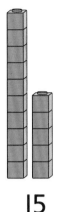  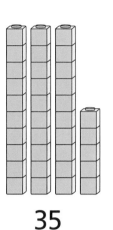 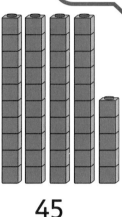 

15	25	35	45
3	☐	☐	☐

S Fill in the missing numbers.

$5 \div 5 = \boxed{}$ $30 \div 5 = \boxed{}$ $45 \div 5 = \boxed{}$

$20 \div 5 = \boxed{}$ $60 \div 5 = \boxed{}$ $40 \div 5 = \boxed{}$

D Fill in the missing numbers. Then colour each of these numbers on the cube. Use a different colour for each number.

$\boxed{} \div 5 = 2$ $\boxed{} \div 5 = 7$

$\boxed{} \div 5 = 5$ $\boxed{} \div 5 = 10$

$\boxed{} \div 5 = 8$ $\boxed{} \div 5 = 11$

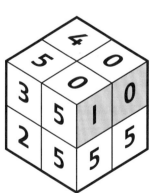

Circle the multiples of 2 and shade the multiples of 5.

16	13	15	35	22
8	9	5	2	55
7	12	18	21	37
1	45	27	25	6

Multiples of 2 are even. Multiples of 5 end in 0 or 5.

Can you think of any numbers that are multiples of both 2 and 5?

 Write a ×2 and a ×5 fact for each door number.

[ ] × 2

[ ] × 5

 20

[ ] × 2

[ ] × 5

 10

Which is my door? My house number is: less than 7 × 5, greater than 11 × 2, not equal to 6 × 5. Tick my door.

 20

 30

 36

 21

 25

☐ ☐ ☐ ☐ ☐

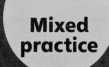

Mixed tables

T Tick if both answers are the same.

2 × 10   10 × 2   2 × 5   5 × 5

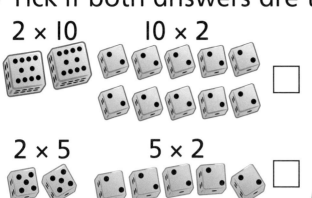 □ □

2 × 5   5 × 2   10 × 5   5 × 10

□ □

S Colour the answers to the multiplications to show the sheep a route through the maze. Work out the top row of multiplications first. Start each row on the left.

8 × 2	3 × 5	12 × 2	4 × 5	9 × 5	1 × 10
10 × 10	8 × 5	7 × 5	2 × 5	7 × 10	5 × 5

30	6	22	43	14	5	18	49
12	24	20	37	29	21	19	18
16	15	45	25	8	10	70	25
23	2	10	100	40	35	4	41

D Which numbers in the maze are not multiples of 2, 5 or 10?

_____

_____

How do you know?

Bingo

T Complete the table.

	×2	×5	×10
6	12		
7			
9			

Multiply each number on the left side of the grid by 2, by 5 and by 10.

S Colour the answers on the Bingo cards.
Which card gets three in a line to win?

20 ÷ 2   5 × 5   10 × 10   35 ÷ 5   9 × 5   16 ÷ 2

8 × 5   30 ÷ 5   11 × 5   40 ÷ 10   12 × 2

BINGO

8	9	100
80	120	4
25	35	22

BINGO

10	45	24
7	160	30
15	40	80

BINGO

40	50	102
6	101	30
5	14	55

☐   ☐   ☐

D Write one ÷2, ÷5 or ÷10 fact for each number on the Bingo card.

BINGO

3	9	1
7	8	6
5	11	15

6 ÷ 2		

Super stars

 Circle groups of stars to show each multiplication.

$$10 = 5 \times 2 \qquad 10 = 2 \times 5$$

Group in 2s for the first one.

 Write two multiplication facts for each set of numbers.

8
4 2

$\boxed{} \times \boxed{} = \boxed{}$

$\boxed{} \times \boxed{} = \boxed{}$

$\boxed{} \times \boxed{} = \boxed{}$

$\boxed{} \times \boxed{} = \boxed{}$

50
10 5

Swap the numbers around to help you.

20
10 2

$\boxed{} \times \boxed{} = \boxed{}$

$\boxed{} \times \boxed{} = \boxed{}$

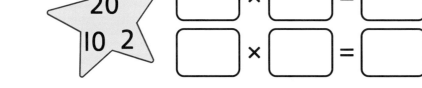 Write the answer to the multiplications.

$2 \times 3 = \boxed{}$

$10 \times 4 = \boxed{}$

$5 \times 4 = \boxed{}$

$10 \times 8 = \boxed{}$

$5 \times 9 = \boxed{}$

$2 \times 7 = \boxed{}$

Problem puzzles

T Write the answers to the questions.

What is 7 times 2? 14

How many 5s make 15? ☐

What is 12 multiplied by 10? ☐

30 is made from how many 10s? ☐

24 is how many 2s? ☐

How many 5s are in 45? ☐

S Write a calculation and answer for each problem.

Each car holds 5 children. How many children are in 7 cars?

10 pencils are in each box. How many boxes hold 110 pencils in total?

_____   _____

D Write a puzzle or draw a picture to match each number fact.

$8 \times 2 = 16$ $40 \div 5 = 8$

Fact action

 Write a ×2, ×5 or ×10 fact for each pile of coins.

 = 10p 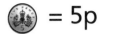 = 5p  = 2p

$\boxed{7} \times 2 = \boxed{}$ $\boxed{} \times \boxed{} = \boxed{}$ $\boxed{} \times \boxed{} = \boxed{}$

 Fill in the missing numbers.

11 × 5 = $\boxed{}$	$\boxed{}$ × 5 = 40	1 × $\boxed{}$ = 10
$\boxed{}$ × 2 = 18	10 × $\boxed{}$ = 50	$\boxed{}$ × 5 = 45
30 ÷ 5 = $\boxed{}$	$\boxed{}$ ÷ 5 = 10	$\boxed{}$ ÷ 2 = 1
$\boxed{}$ ÷ 2 = 10	10 ÷ $\boxed{}$ = 5	14 ÷ $\boxed{}$ = 7

Write some ÷5 facts using the digits 0, 1, 2 and 5. The first number in the division sentences must be 50 or greater. You can use each digit more than once.

_____ _____ _____

_____ _____ _____

_____ _____ _____

Quiz time

 T Write the answers to the multiplications.

2 × 2 = **4**	5 × 5 = ☐	1 × 10 = ☐
11 × 5 = ☐	8 × 10 = ☐	7 × 5 = ☐
7 × 10 = ☐	9 × 5 = ☐	12 × 2 = ☐

 S Fill in the missing numbers.

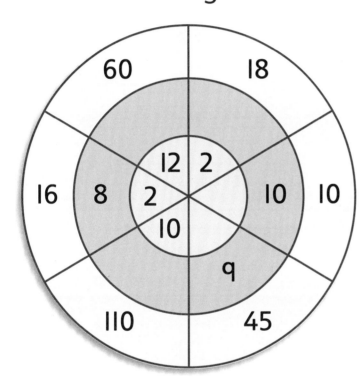

Divide the outer numbers to find the inner numbers.

 D Complete the rhyme. Make up your own rhyme to help you remember a different fact.

Hip, hop,
I like to jive!
Nine times five
is _____-five!

_____

_____

_____

_____

Finding new facts

 T Find double 14 in different ways.

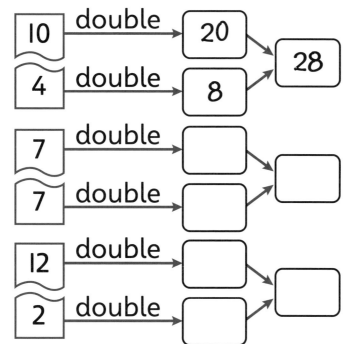

10	double →	20	
4	double →	8	→ 28
7	double →	☐	
7	double →	☐	→ ☐
12	double →	☐	
2	double →	☐	→ ☐

Split 14 into two parts. Double each part and add the answers.

 S Fill in the missing numbers.

17 × 5

10 × 5 = 50

7 × 5 = 35

17 × 5 = ☐

13 × 5

10 × 5 = ☐

3 × 5 = ☐

13 × 5 = ☐

19 × 5

☐ × 5 = ☐

☐ × 5 = ☐

19 × 5 = ☐

D Join pairs with the same answer. What patterns do you notice?

16 × 5 = ☐   14 × 5 = ☐

18 × 5 = ☐   9 × 10 = ☐

7 × 10 = ☐   8 × 10 = ☐

Practice makes perfect

 Write a multiplication for each addition.

| 2 | +2 | +2 | +2 | +2 | +2 | +2 |

[ ] × [2] = [ ]

| 10 | +10 | +10 | +10 | +10 |

[ ] × [ ] = [ ]

| 5 | +5 | +5 | +5 | +5 | +5 |

[ ] × [ ] = [ ]

 Put a **circle** around multiples of 2. Put a **square** around multiples of 5. Put a **triangle** around multiples of 10.

5   6   7   8   9   10   11   12

13   14   15   16   17   18   20

Why do some numbers have all three shapes?

 (D) Multiply each number by 2, 5 and 10. Then order the answers (smallest first).

 6

 1

 4

 9

6 × 2 = [12]   _____ _____ _____

6 × 5 = [ ]   _____ _____ _____

6 × 10 = [ ]   _____ _____ _____

31

pinpoint MATHS

times tables detectives

This book provides practice for the **2, 5 and 10 times tables**.

The activities focus on reasoning and applying as well as fluent recall, so that children's times tables equip them for success in maths as a whole. Each page contains a Towards, Securing and Deeper section, encouraging children to spot patterns and think in greater depth – like a times tables detective!

The free online *Pinpoint Times Tables Check* can be used alongside this book: **www.pearsonprimary.co.uk/ttcheck**

Find out more about *Pinpoint* materials at: **www.pearsonprimary.co.uk/pinpoint**

Published by Pearson Education Limited, 80 Strand, London, WC2R 0RL

www.pearsonschools.co.uk

Text and original illustrations © Pearson Education Limited 2019
Written by Hilary Koll and Steve Mills
Edited by Just Content
Typeset by PDQ
Characters illustrated by The Boy Fitz Hammond
Cover design by Pearson Education Limited
Coins and bank notes page 13, 17, 28, Crown Copyright: The Royal Mint, © Crown Copyright. Contains public sector information licensed under the Open Government Licence v3.0

The right of Hilary Koll and Steve Mills to be identified as authors of this work has been asserted by them in accordance with the Copyright, Designs and Patents Act 1988.

First published 2019

22 21 20 19
10 9 8 7 6 5 4 3 2 1

British Library Cataloguing in Publication Data
A catalogue record for this book is available from the British Library
ISBN 978 1 292 29101 7

Printed in Slovakia by Neografia

Note from the publisher
Pearson is not liable for any misunderstandings that arise as a result of errors in this publication, but it is our priority to ensure that the content is accurate. If you spot an error, please do contact us at resourcescorrections@pearson.com so we can make sure it is corrected.

Year 2: England & Wales
Primary 3: Scotland & Northern Ireland

www.pearsonschools.co.uk
myorders@pearson.com

ISBN 978-1-292-29101-7

9 781292 291017